W9-AEC-577

Basketball
ABC
The NBA Alphabet

Florence Cassen Mayers

Harry N. Abrams, Inc.
Publishers

For John and Anthony Schiff,
with special thanks for their great assists

Editor: Sharon AvRutick
Designer: Florence Cassen Mayers

Library of Congress Catalog Card Number: 95–78670
ISBN 0–8109–3143–5

Published in 1996 by Harry N. Abrams, Incorporated, New York
A Times Mirror Company

Printed and bound in Hong Kong

Introduction

Want to know what size **Shoe** Shaquille O'Neal wears? Look up **S**. Under **H** see Gheorghe Muresan and Muggsy Bogues, and find out the average **Height** of NBA players. **L** is for **Legends** where you get Wilt "the Stilt" Chamberlain, Kareem Abdul-Jabbar, and nine other superstars. Speaking of superstars, check out **Dream Team**, under **D**. Michael Jordan takes to the air on the **J** page. **M**'s for **Mascots**, **R**'s for **Rebound**, **K**'s for **Key**. Pages are packed with brilliant color action photos, weird-angle overhead shots, and detailed close-ups you miss in the heat of the game.

Basketball ABC: The NBA Alphabet celebrates basketball. Readers will include anyone who's watched the playoffs on TV, and anyone who's been to a game. It's designed both to intrigue knowledgeable fans and excite your Aunt Tillie, who hardly knows the difference between Michael Jordan and Michael Jackson. It may even help the little kids you know learn their ABCs. Is this a book for kids? Sure. But I've also made it for their moms, dads, grandpas, grandmas, aunts, and uncles.

F.C.M.

Arena

Where the game is played. The Alamodome, home of the
San Antonio Spurs, is filled with a capacity crowd of more than 34,000
screaming fans cheering on their team.

B

Basketball

The official NBA ball measures 9 inches in diameter, weighs 20–22 ounces, and is inflated to between 7½ and 8½ pounds of pressure.

Basket

The 18-inch metal ring is strung with a white cord net 15 to 18 inches long, mounted just 10 feet above the floor—though on some nights it can seem like 10 miles.

b

Block

The sound of
a clean blocked
shot—the slap
of hand against
leather—echoes
throughout the
arena.

Court

All you need is a backboard and a hoop on the side of a garage or even in the midst of a cornfield. The game's played every day, everywhere across the country, in city schoolyards and in fishing villages.

Dream Team

Left to right:
Christian Laettner,
Patrick Ewing,
David Robinson *(behind Ewing)*,
Larry Bird,
Scottie Pippen,
Michael Jordan,
Clyde Drexler,
Karl Malone,
John Stockton,
Chris Mullin,
Charles Barkley,
and Magic Johnson
were a nightmare for every
team they met in the 1992
Summer Olympics, and they
brought home the gold.

Dunk

For most of us it's just a
fantasy, but for the likes of
Shaquille O'Neal, leaping
up and slamming the ball
in over the top of the rim
is only everyday heroics.

Eastern Conference

f F

Free throw

Standing alone, all eyes on him, the crowd's scream resounding in his ears, Chris Mullin focuses on that extra point. The best free throw shooters make over ninety percent of their shots.

Goal

Basket! Bucket!
Two pointer! Trey!
It's a swish!

Height

Gheorghe Muresan—7'7".
Muggsy Bogues—5'4".
And in between, the
average NBA player—6'7".

Inbounds pass

After a moment of stillness, the ball is thrown back into play—and the game goes on.

J j
ump shot

He leaves his feet, he elevates, he hangs in the air! He's Michael Jordan, defying gravity!

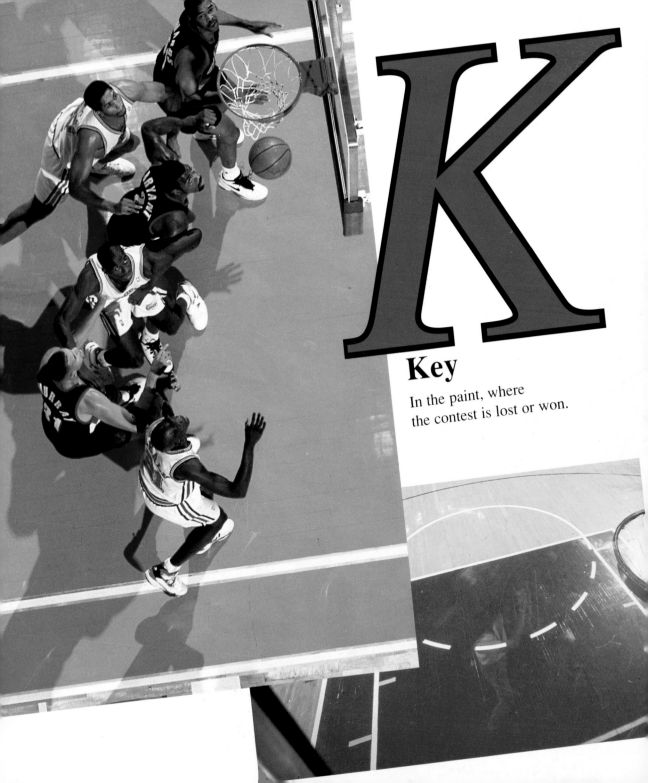

K

Key

In the paint, where
the contest is lost or won.

Wilt Chamberlain
1959–73
Philadelphia Warriors
San Francisco Warriors
Los Angeles Lakers

Julius Erving
1971–87
Virginia Squires
New York Nets
Philadelphia 76ers

Jerry West
1960–74
Los Angeles Lakers

George Mikan
1946–56
Chicago Stags
Minneapolis Lakers

Larry Bird
1979–92
Boston Celtics

Kareem Abdul-Jabbar
1969–89
Milwaukee Bucks
Los Angeles Lakers

L

Legends

The all-time greats, the seasons they played, and their teams.

Michael Jordan
1984–93, 1995–
Chicago Bulls

Bob Cousy
1950–70
Boston Celtics
Cincinnati Royals

Oscar Robertson
1960–74
Cincinnati Royals
Milwaukee Bucks

Magic Johnson
1979–91, '96–
Los Angeles Lakers

Bill Russell
1956–69
Boston Celtics

Mascots

Beloved by children
and adults alike for
their antics, which
include putting jinxes
on the opposing team.

M

Hugo
Charlotte
Hornets

Squatch
Seattle Sonics

The Coyote
San Antonio
Spurs

Rocky
Denver
Nuggets

Benny
Chicago Bulls

unch
nnesota
mberwolves

m

Nn

Dr. James Naismith

A teacher at a YMCA school in Springfield, Massachusetts, Naismith invented basketball in 1891 when he had two peach baskets nailed to the balcony of the gym.

One on one

Julius Erving and a competitor demonstrate
the essence of basketball. Offensive and defensive
skills are tested and refined in this contest.

Palm

Players can grab a basketball the way you or I would hold a relatively small cantaloupe.

Quote

Qq

"I never thought I'd lead the NBA in rebounding, but I got a lot of help from my teammates. They did a lot of missing."

—Moses Malone

"My biggest thrill came the night Elgin [Baylor] and I combined for 73 points in Madison Square Garden. Elgin had 71 of them."

—Hot Rod Hundley

Referee

Coaches, players, fans, and the refs don't always see eye to eye. Here the ref—there are 3 in every game—signals a pushing foul.

Going for the ball, they box out, they crash the boards. Wilt Chamberlain holds the all-time NBA record with 23,924 career rebounds.

Rebound

r

Shoe

Shaquille O'Neal wears size 22. At 16½ inches it's almost 5 inches longer than the average man's size 10.

SkyBox ROOKIE HILL

94-95

DAVID ROBINSON
CENTER NBA HOOPS

MOOKIE BLAYLOCK

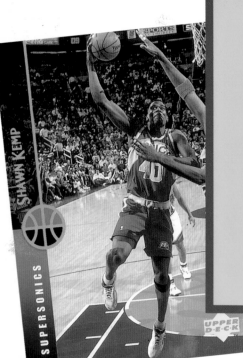

SHAWN KEMP

SUPERSONICS

UPPER DECK

t

FLEER '94

ABOUT TH

LARRY JOHNSON
CHARLOTTE HORNETS • F

T

Trading cards

If your mother doesn't throw them away, maybe you'll give them to *your* kids someday.

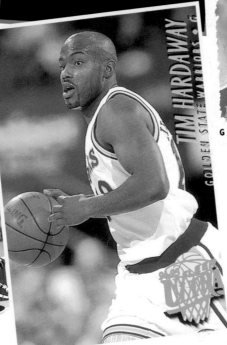

u

Uniform

The 1996 NBA All-Star jerseys. These special jerseys are redesigned and updated every year.

Victory

What it's all about.

Western Conference

It's time out.
The game's coming to a close.
The coach maps out a strategy
using X's and O's.
Each X represents an offensive player,
and each O is a defender.

DETROIT
PISTONS

DETROIT
PISTONS

DENVER
NUGGETS

OFFICIAL 19

$6.95

HOUSTON ROCKETS

HOUSTON
ROCKETS

OFFICIAL 1994-95 TEAM YEARBOOK

1993-94
NBA
WORLD
CHAMPIONS

HOUSTON
34

$6.95

1994
1995
NEW JERSEY NETS

Official Yearbook   Official Yearbook $6.95

NETS
7

Yearbooks

Yy

Packed with info about your
favorite teams—rosters, player
stats and biographies, action
photos, season highlights.

Z

Zero

Players choose their own numbers. Many stick with the number they wore in college throughout their entire NBA careers.

Photograph Credits
All photographs courtesy of NBA Photos. (left to right)
Front cover: D. Clarke Evans (arena), NBA Photos/NBA
Photo Library (Wilt Chamberlain), David Kyle/NBA Photos
(ball), Sam Forencich (Denver mascot), Rocky Widner
(Patrick Ewing). Back cover: Nathaniel S. Butler (rebound),
Gregg Forwerck (Charlotte Hornet), Andrew D. Bernstein
(key). Introduction: Nathaniel S. Butler/NBA Photos.
A: D. Clarke Evans. B: Andrew D. Bernstein, Nathaniel S.
Butler. C: Nathaniel S. Butler (all). D: Andrew D. Bernstein,
Barry Gossage. F: Tim Defrisco. G: Andrew D. Bernstein.
H: Lou Capozzola, Andrew D. Bernstein. I: Jon Hayt.
J: Nathaniel S. Butler. K: Andrew D. Bernstein, Scott
Cunningham. L: NBA Photos/NBA Photo Library (Jerry
West, Wilt Chamberlain, Bob Cousy, George Mikan, Bill
Russell, Oscar Robertson), Andrew D. Bernstein/NBA
Photos (Julius Erving, Michael Jordan, Magic Johnson),
Nathaniel S. Butler/NBA Photos (Larry Bird), Andrew D.
Bernstein/NBA Photos (Kareem Abdul-Jabbar). M: Jeff
Reinking (Seattle), Tommy Hultgren (San Antonio), Gregg
Forwerck (Charlotte), Nathaniel S. Butler, (Minnesota),
Noren Trotman (Chicago), Sam Forencich (Denver).
N: NBA Photo Library. O: Andrew D. Bernstein. P: Brian
Drake. R: Nathaniel S. Butler, Andrew D. Bernstein.
S: Barry Gossage, Steven Freeman. T: Courtesy of Fleer,
SkyBox, Upper Deck, and Topps trading card companies.
U: Steven Freeman. V: Andrew D. Bernstein. X: Andrew D.
Bernstein/NBA Photos. Y: Courtesy of Sports Media, Inc.
Z: Rocky Widner.